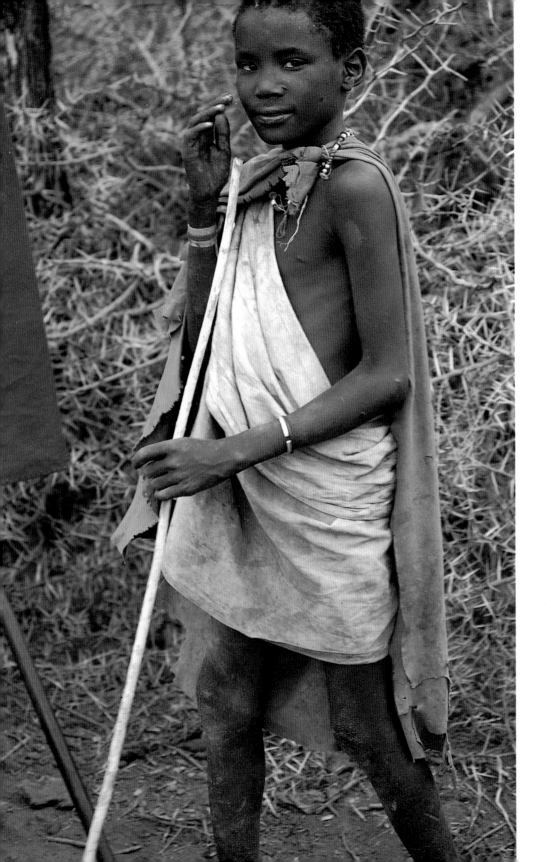

Olbalbal

A DAY IN MAASAILAND

BARBARA A. MARGOLIES

FOUR WINDS PRESS ❖ New York

MAXWELL MACMILLAN CANADA Toronto

MAXWELL MACMILLAN INTERNATIONAL New York Oxford Singapore Sydney

For Ira, Ilisa, and Gregory

—B.A.M.

Four Winds Press
Macmillan Publishing Company
866 Third Avenue
New York, NY 10022

Maxwell Macmillan Canada, Inc.
1200 Eglinton Avenue East
Suite 200
Don Mills, Ontario M3C 3N1

Macmillan Publishing Company is part of the
Maxwell Communication Group of Companies.

First edition
Printed and bound in Hong Kong
10 9 8 7 6 5 4 3 2 1

The text of this book is set in Meridien.
Book design by Christy Hale
Map by Jeanyee Wong
Some of the names of the Maasai who live in Olbalbal have been changed.

Library of Congress Cataloging-in-Publication Data
Margolies, Barbara A., date.
Olbalbal : a day in Maasailand / Barbara A. Margolies.—1st ed.
     p.   cm.
Summary: Text and photographs describe life in a Masai village in
Tanzania.
ISBN 0-02-762284-3
1. Masai (African people)—Juvenile literature. [1. Masai
(African people)] I. Title.
DT443.3.M37M37   1994
967.62'004965—dc20   93-19744

I would like to thank His Excellency, Ambassador A. B.
Nyakyi; Professor Alan H. Jacobs, Department of Anthro-
pology, Western Michigan University, Kalamazoo; and
William Meiliari, internationally known guide and lecturer
for Abercrombie & Kent, Tanzania, for reading my manu-
script. Many thanks as well to Lion's Safari International for
arrangements in Maasailand, and to Edward Sindato ole
Ngobei, lecturer for Ngorongoro Sopa Lodge.

A note to readers: In *Maa*, the language of the Maasai,
Olbalbal is a noun meaning "pond," "pool," "temporary
lake," or "deep pit."

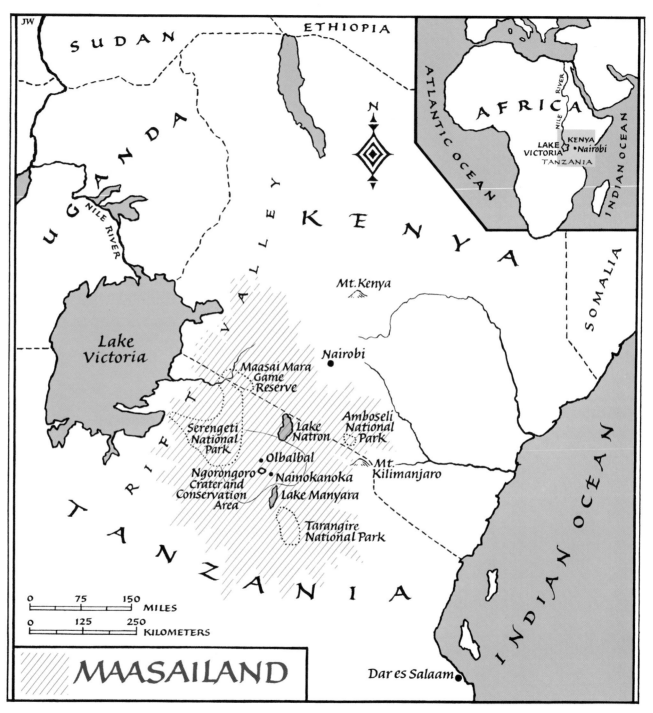

The Maasai are seminomadic. They sometimes move back and forth across the unmarked boundaries of Maasailand.

This book chronicles a day in the village of Olbalbal, Tanzania. The lifestyles and customs presented on these pages may vary from those in the other Maasai villages scattered across Maasailand.

I think of Africa often: the sweet smell of wet grass after the rains; the sight of a magnificent rainbow reaching across the sky; the strange sound of the wind blowing through the "whistling thorn" bushes that grow on the African plains. And I think of all the handsome and proud Maasai people I have met on my many trips to Tanzania.

I had been with the people of Olbalbal for several days when a young Maasai woman took me behind her house. I was puzzled. She slid her robe off her shoulder and showed me the welts from a beating by her husband. I gently touched her bruised skin; she smiled. It was then I realized that despite our cultural differences and lack of a common language, we—as women—were able to establish a bond that allowed us to share significant moments throughout my stay.

With great joy, I remember another Maasai woman who took my hand and urged me to join her as she began to run to a house—a baby had just been born! The women of Olbalbal gathered to sing a song to their god, EnKai, welcoming the child. And I was part of this celebration of life.

Understandably, many Maasai are afraid of change, afraid of altering a way of life that has been tradition for so long. A Maasai friend, William Meiliari, writes from Tanzania about his people: "Knowing that education brings change, many Maasai have avoided sending their children to school. They fear that education will turn our children away from our customs and culture. Many think that if our children go to school, they will not want to come back to the village. Instead, they will move to the cities and find employment there. They will not speak the Maasai language; they will be lost forever. I think that many Maasai now realize it is time for progress, time for development. Hopefully, we will be able to preserve many of our traditions as we go forward."

The winds of change have already begun to blow across Maasailand. Miles away from Olbalbal, in the village of Nainokanoka, changes have already taken place. The children there told me about the schools they attend and about the nearby medical clinic. Even the younger children eagerly spoke of becoming teachers and doctors—dreams of the future.

Someday I will return to Africa. Probably I will be saddened for the old ways that have been left behind and joyful for what is new. Indeed, Africa has become a part of me, now and always.

B.A.M.

The *Wamasai** of Kenya and Tanzania probably number no more than 500,000. This is the size of several of the smaller ethnic groups among the more than 120 that make up Tanzania. Yet, they are, without question, one of the best-known groups among the peoples of East Africa. What has fascinated many people in the West about the *Wamasai* is their continuing attachment to their seminomadic way of life. To the countries where the *Wamasai* live, the need to reconcile this way of life with the needs and benefits of modern life has always posed a dilemma.

The photographs and text in this book present a day in a traditional Masai village. I trust they will enable the reader to understand and appreciate not just the beauty and majesty of the *Wamasai*, but also the problems they have to overcome in everyday life.

A. B. Nyakyi
Ambassador
Permanent Representative
of Tanzania
to the United Nations

* In Kiswahili, the official language of Tanzania, the prefix "Wa" means "people of." *Wamasai* means "people of the Masai."

The Maasai live on the open plains of East Africa. It is believed that the Maasai people originally came from northeastern Africa more than four hundred years ago. Perhaps due to famine or drought, they moved southward, and eventually settled on the grasslands of Kenya and Tanzania.

The Maasai speak a language they call *Maa*. They worship one god, EnKai, whom they believe gave them cattle as a gift to be treasured. Historically, the Maasai did not cultivate crops, hunt, or gather wild food. They were a seminomadic people who tried to live solely off the milk, meat, and blood of their livestock. Like other East Africa peoples, Maasai warriors sometimes went on cattle raids against neighboring tribes. Sometimes, the Maasai were raided by their neighbors. But the Maasai's reputation as a fierce and warring nation was often deliberately exaggerated, first by Arab slave and ivory traders in order to discourage Europeans from exploring the interior of East Africa, and later by colonial powers in order to justify their taking land away from the Maasai.

left
Clouds settling on the rim of Ngorongoro Crater. Once a volcano, the crater was created when the sudden withdrawal of molten lava caused the center to collapse. The floor of the crater became home to wild animals, and to the Maasai and their cattle. A number of years ago, conservation authorities moved the Maasai out of the crater, leaving it solely to the animals.

above
Children play on the open plains of Maasailand. Traditionally, Maasai girls take care of their younger sisters and brothers.

7

In the 1920s, the ruling British colonial government began to put restrictions on the Maasai, including a ban on cattle raiding. This ban continued even after Tanzania and Kenya became independent nations in the early 1960s.

Some Maasai, including the Tanzanian Maasai pictured in this book, continue to live a seminomadic life. Their lives are still dependent on their cattle. They build their houses where the grass is plentiful and water is available for their herds. When the grass is gone, they abandon their homes, take their families and possessions, and move on to find new food for their animals. For these traditional Maasai, their cattle determine their wealth and status in the community, as well as provide their main source of food.

below
Maasai men, women, and children gather to count their herds and to check for disease. All herds are marked or branded to distinguish each family's animals.

right
A herdsboy with his cattle. Alone on the plains, he carries a herding stick and a short spear for protection from wild animals.

The warm winds blow across the vast plains of Maasailand. Dust rises in ghostly whirls and then disappears in the air. Clouds encircle the surrounding mountaintops. The African sun is hot, and a lion searches for shade under the branches of a tree.

Scattered throughout the huge Ngorongoro Conservation Area are hundreds of Maasai villages. In one of these villages, the village of Olbalbal, lives Kisululu, a six-year-old Maasai boy. Kisululu lives with his parents and brothers and sisters in a house built by his mother. On either side of Kisululu's house live his father's other wives and their children. Close by are Kisululu's father's parents.

below

Kisululu (left) and friend. Maasai children are often sick with stomach parasites; trachoma, an eye infection that can lead to blindness; upper respiratory tract infections; and malaria.

above
Children outside their house. In each house, there is a small opening in the roof or wall. The opening allows smoke from a continually smoldering fire inside to escape.

left
Women gather to talk. Maasai men may have a number of wives, and each wife builds her own house. Before a new house is occupied, it must be blessed by the elders.

The Maasai women build all of the houses in the village. The houses are made of sticks and grass and are covered with cow dung. Inside, the family members sleep on beds of woven branches. The branches are cushioned with dry grass and covered with animal skins. It can get very cold during the night, and Kisululu's mother often puts extra skin blankets on him. For added warmth, she keeps a small fire burning in the middle of the house.

A Maasai village is called an *enkang*. The men put a thick wall of dried thorn-tree branches around the circle of houses. These thorn branches prevent wild animals from coming into the *enkang*. But nothing can keep out the snakes! Deadly snakes such as cobras, puff adders, and black mambas sometimes crawl into the *enkang*. Just like all Maasai children, Kisululu is very frightened of snakes. If a child is bitten, his or her mother will quickly cut the surrounding area, suck out the poison, and put a piece of herbal bark from a tree on the wound.

The Maasai tell the time of day by the position of the sun in the sky, and the time of month by the shape of the moon. Kisululu's day begins when the sun fills the eastern sky. His mother collects wood for the fire. She mixes cornmeal and milk for the morning meal. Sometimes, she finds wild berries for her family.

The Maasai drink the milk from their cows or goats every day. When they don't have enough milk, they mix cow's blood with the milk. To get the blood, Maasai men shoot an arrow into the jugular vein in a cow's neck. The blood spills into a gourd. To stop the flow of blood, a wad of dung and mud is packed into the arrow hole. The cow is then returned to the herd. The Maasai believe that blood makes them strong. At special celebrations, a cow is killed and the whole village shares the roasted meat.

far left
Woman stirring blood in a gourd. Maasai women work together to provide everyday needs for the whole village.

left
Kisululu and friends enjoy some milk. Because the Maasai share their living space with their cattle, there are always many, many flies in the area. The children are accustomed to flies all over their clothing and faces.

above
Woman feeding her baby ghee, the fat of cow's milk. The ghee is stored in the horn resting on the mother's leg.

15

After the morning meal, Kisululu's mother and aunts clean animal skins and put them out to dry in the sun. The skins are softened with animal fat and some are colored with red ocher, a mineral from the earth. The women sit together and talk while they sew and decorate the skins with beads. They teach the young girls to bead, too.

Maasai woman sewing beads on a skin. Traditional dress includes many arm and leg bracelets. Even babies wear leather amulets to ward off evil spirits.

Kisululu likes to watch his mother sew. Her fingers move so fast!

A Maasai girl unrolls a "finished" skin. She will sit on it while she beads with her mother.

Animal skins are put out to dry in the sun. Wooden sticks are used to stretch the smaller skins.

This woman has completed an elaborate design on a cowhide.

She will use the hide as a skirt worn only for special celebrations.

Showing off her beautiful necklace, this Maasai woman also wears wide, bead-covered earrings to show she is married. Since Maasai regard hair as a symbol of assertiveness, it is traditional for Maasai women to shave their heads as a sign of respect.

Maasai women work very hard during the day. One of their chores is to pick calabashes, or gourds, from vines. They clean out the insides of the gourds and put the gourds in the sun to dry, just like the animal skins. The women decorate the dried gourds with beads and leather. Milk, blood, water, and cornmeal are stored inside the gourds. Delicious honey, collected from beehives, is also kept in the gourds. Sometimes, Maasai children are allowed to stick their fingers into the honey and eat as much as they want.

left
A Maasai woman pours milk into a large gourd. The Maasai use burning embers from wild olive trees to clean out gourds. Milk stored in those gourds will have a smoky taste.

Some mornings, the women leave the *enkang* with their donkeys. They walk many miles, over rocky paths and through thick bush, to a faraway water pipe, built just for the Maasai. If the rains haven't come yet and the streams are all dried up, the new pipe is the only place to find water. Donkeys carry gourds filled with water back to the *enkang*.

One day, a lion killed one of the donkeys. Kisululu was very frightened for his mother. Who would help her if the lion came again? Kisululu's father and the other elders went out into the bush looking for the lion, but they could not find him.

Kisululu's father is teaching him to identify lion, cheetah, and leopard footprints. When he is older, Kisululu will be able to help the warriors track down the animals that attack their donkeys and cattle. And he'll be able to protect his mother, too.

A village grandmother, Nanginyi, plays a game with the children. When Maasai children are very young, they are taught to respect all their elders.

Two boys being scolded. If a child has misbehaved, he or she may be scolded by any of the adults in the village, not just the child's parents. If a child has done something good, he or she will be rewarded with milk or a good piece of meat at celebration time.

Sometimes during the day, Kisululu likes to play with his sister Engogko and his cousins. A village grandmother plays with the children, too, and she tells them old stories of the Maasai. Today, Kisululu's friends Loiruk and Lukmai are not allowed to play. They are being scolded because they went far away from the *enkang* and their mother didn't know where they were. They could have been attacked by a lion, and no one would have heard their cries for help.

Chief Lemeikoke ole Ngiyaa tells the children that he played the same games when he was young. And he tended his father's herds just as the boys of this village do.

These days, things are changing for the Maasai of Olbalbal. Tanzanian farmers need land to grow their crops. As farms expand, Maasai cattle will have fewer places to graze. Without their cattle, the Maasai cannot live as they have for so long. The government plans to build schools and teach Maasai children to read and write. Some Maasai will leave the village for the city. The Maasai way of life will change and the Maasai people will change, too.

below

Chief Lemeikoke ole Ngiyaa talks with the children. He is the "chief" of his people and is considered a very wise man. Ole Ngiyaa has eight wives, sixty-four children, and so many grandchildren that he forgets their names! Elders like ole Ngiyaa keep the Maasai culture and traditions alive by telling stories to the children.

Warriors gather the children to sing to EnKai. Maasai children are also taught many songs about their cattle. The songs emphasize the importance of the cattle to the Maasai.

A Maasai girl sings to EnKai. Girls as young as thirteen are ready for marriage in Maasai tradition. The husbands are much older than the young brides, and each husband must pay a dowry to the bride's parents. The dowry might consist of cows, tobacco, honey, and sheepskins.

In the dry season, when the grasses are parched and brown, the cattle become thin and sometimes sickly, and they cannot produce enough milk for the Maasai to drink. Then Kisululu and the other children gather to sing to their god, EnKai, asking him to bring the rains.

The elders and the women also pray to EnKai. The women dress in their finest skins, and accompanied by two men with a lamb, they walk to a nearby mountaintop. There, the men, also dressed in their best skins, slaughter the lamb and offer it to EnKai. The women carry gourds filled with honey and milk. They mix the honey and milk with the blood of the lamb, they say a blessing, and they sprinkle the liquid around the area where the lamb has been killed. The women sing many songs asking EnKai for rain.

This girl's earlobes have been cut and stretched with wads of grass. Now wooden plugs are used to make the lobes even bigger. It is a sign of beauty to have long, stretched earlobes. The decorative cuts on her face are also signs of beauty.

25

Maasai males live in three life stages—childhood, warriorhood, and elderhood. Each stage has specific duties and responsibilities. Elders are the traditional heads of their families. They make all the decisions, judge quarrels, and solve problems in the village. They also go to the markets to sell the cattle and to buy beads, cornmeal, and cloth for the women. The elders are responsible for organizing and leading celebrations and ceremonies.

Maasai boys spend their days caring for the family cattle, goats, and sheep. When boys are six or seven, they begin to take the herds out to graze. If a lion or a leopard comes near the herd, a herdsboy must yell and shout to chase the wild animal away. When a boy cannot protect the herd himself, he must run, as fast as he can, back to the village for help.

below
A herdsboy stands guard over his cattle. He must always look for lions or leopards that might try to attack his animals. And he must be very careful not to step on snakes that are curled in the grass.

left
A Maasai boy tends his herds on the plains. From June to October, the grasses begin to dry. The short rains begin in November, and the heavy rains fall in April and May.

When Maasai boys turn fifteen or sixteen, they take part in a special ceremony that initiates them into manhood. After the ceremony, the new warriors, or *murrans,* wear blackened cloth and paint their faces. The proud *murrans* make their own headpieces out of birds and feathers and wood.

The *murrans* go to a special feasting camp called *Olpul.* The camp is usually far away from the village, and the *murrans* stay there for a month or more. There, the *murrans* gain strength from feasting on meat, pray to EnKai, and learn the traditional ways.

far left

New warriors wear beaded belts and rings given to them by their girlfriends. The ceremony that initiates them into manhood, or warriorhood, is called *Emorata* in the Maasai language. This ceremony is one of the most important times in a Maasai male's life.

left

A warrior shows off his headpiece. The birds used in this headpiece were first cleaned and stuffed with ashes and dried grass and then attached to this horseshoe-shaped crown.

Kisululu's brother Tubiko has been a *murran* for five years. He is very tall and strong. In this village, the warriors grow their hair very long and put red ocher in it. Much of the beautiful jewelry they wear is given to them by their many girlfriends. They are not allowed to marry while they are *murrans*. A long time ago, when Chief Lemeikoke ole Ngiyaa was a *murran*, the warriors went on cattle raids and fought other tribes. Stories about brave and clever Maasai warriors and the fierce battles they fought are told again and again to young children.

Today, the Maasai do not fight wars and there are not many cattle raids. The *murrans* are responsible for finding new sources of water and food for the herds.

above

A warrior, or *murran*, shows off his father's headpiece of ostrich feathers. In the past, warriors would wear headpieces like this one when they went into battle.

right

These *murrans* paint each other's hair with ocher. Sometimes cotton or wool threads are added to the hair to make it very long. The *murrans* spend a lot of time beautifying themselves. They will spend about seven years as junior warriors and then another seven as senior warriors. At the end of this period, the warriors become elders in a special ceremony called *Olng'esherr*.

The *murrans* still practice using their spears because they must be ready to protect their village from wild animals. Kisululu likes to watch the warriors. He knows it will take years of practice before he is as strong and brave as Tubiko.

As the sun begins to set in the west, the Maasai boys come home, bringing in the herds of cattle, goats, and sheep. The entire village gathers to help. The animals must be counted before the sun turns red. The mothers milk the goats and cows so that everyone will have an evening meal. Kisululu helps to bring his father's animals inside the *enkang*. As darkness comes, the men pull thick thorn-tree branches across the entrances to Olbalbal. Now the Maasai are safe from the wild animals.

Perhaps Kisululu will hear more stories from the elders tonight. Finally, he will fall asleep, under blankets of skins, listening to the hyenas and the distant roars of lions.